SUBTLE ENGINEERING

HOW MODERN SAAS TEAMS SHIP FAST, STAY SANE, AND SKIP THE PROCESS THEATRE

LUKASZ OLCZYK

Subtle Engineering: How Modern SaaS Teams Ship Fast, Stay Sane, and Skip the Process Theatre

ISBN: 978-3-912147-04-9

This work is offered as a reflection, not a prescription. It does not constitute professional advice.

Written with care.

CONTENTS

INTRODUCTION

THE CASE FOR SUBTLE ENGINEERING

I've always found it odd how something as elegant as software delivery can turn into a pantomime.

Stickers on laptops, daily theatrics around "stand-ups," and teams proudly declaring they deploy once a week, as if that's some kind of achievement. It's like celebrating the fact that your postman delivers mail on Thursdays. Only Thursdays.

Let's be clear: this book isn't about trends. It's not about the latest hot framework, nor is it about convincing you that Kubernetes is a lifestyle choice. It's about quiet, consistent, highly competent delivery of software, every day, without making a fuss. It's about Subtle Engineering.

Now, before you roll your eyes and assume I'm here to preach minimalism in a Zen garden, let me be blunt: this isn't soft. It's hard. It's ruthless. It demands discipline, precision, and accountability. But it does so without shouting. Think seasoned field engineer — someone who's seen failure up close, respects reliability, and enjoys debugging both code and carburettors.

But here's the thing: **Subtle Engineering isn't a starting point. It's a destination.**

The systems and habits described in this book — trunk-based development, test ownership, frictionless pipelines, boring deploys — they aren't born overnight. They're built. Slowly. And usually after a few hard lessons. You don't begin here. You grow into it. That growth can be messy, inconsistent, and politically fraught, especially in legacy environments or large, cautious orgs. That's not a flaw. It's the real work.

So if your team still fights merge conflicts, waits for manual QA sign-off, or dreads Friday deploys, this book is still for you. Perhaps especially for you. The pages ahead won't give you a step-by-step transformation plan. What they *will* provide you with is a clear picture of what "better" looks like. Then you can choose how to move toward it: one habit, one toggled feature, one cleaned-up pipeline at a time.

We Move Quietly — But We Ship Constantly

The best software teams I've seen don't talk about Agile. They don't hold retrospectives about how their retrospectives went. They don't argue about which ticketing tool sparks the most joy. They just build. They commit. They test. They deploy several times a day, if needed. And the world keeps turning.

These teams aren't flashy. You won't find them on conference stages with TED-style headset mics. But they're inevitable. Because they've mastered the rhythm of disciplined software creation in 2025.

Why Now?

Over the last decade, two things happened in parallel:

1. Tooling matured. We now have infrastructure that can deploy code faster than people can think up meetings about it.
2. Process ossified. Many teams continued to add layers of ceremony instead of removing friction.

So we ended up with beautifully automated CI/CD pipelines… that no one dares to trust. We have teams that can toggle features in real-time, but they release them monthly, wrapped in PowerPoint. We solved the technical problems and reintroduced the human ones.

Who This Book Is For

If you:

- Lead a software team that's too slow, too noisy, or both
- Want to deploy five times a day without your heart rate spiking
- Are tired of watching ticket boards fill up with process instead of progress
- Believe developers should test, ship, and own what they build

...then this book is for you.

It's also for product managers, engineering leaders, SREs, and founders — anyone who wants their org to ship without the circus. You don't need to be a DevOps sage. You need common sense, clarity, and the courage to remove things instead of adding them.

What to Expect

This book is structured like a field manual — it presents clear principles, specific practices, and no fluff.

We'll cover:

- Trunk-based development as the backbone
- Testing strategies that don't require a separate QA caste
- Feature toggles, rollbacks, and the dark art of boring deployments
- Organisational habits that create quiet, disciplined delivery

Each chapter balances ideas with reality. If you want footnotes from 30 research papers, there are other books. If you want a guide forged in production, run by teams who live in the logs — you're holding it.

Final Thought: Elegance Without Noise

Subtle engineering is about grace under pressure. It's about code that flows, systems that heal themselves, and teams that don't panic. It's not romantic. It's not loud. But it works. Every day. Without fail.

Let's begin, not with perfection, but with direction.

CHAPTER 1
TRUNK-BASED DEVELOPMENT
SHIPPABLE ALWAYS

Let's begin with the aspect that makes every seasoned engineer either nod in approval or break out in hives: **trunk-based development**.

If you've ever found yourself knee-deep in a three-week-old feature branch, resolving merge conflicts at 11:37 p.m. while muttering dark things about Jenkins, then you've already learned the lesson. Possibly the hard way.

The lesson is this: **branches rot.**

CODE IS LIKE MILK, NOT WINE

Some people treat their code like it'll improve with age. Leave it in a branch, let it mature, and test it again next week. Maybe merge it once it's good and ready.

That's not how this works.

The longer the code stays away from the main, the less trustworthy it becomes. It diverges. The surrounding codebase evolves. Integration points shift, behaviours change, and expectations evolve. By the time you're ready to merge, you're trying to retrofit a VHS player into a Tesla.

Your shiny new feature now breaks half the product, and your team is stuck running damage control while the real work gets postponed. Again.

THE RULE IS SIMPLE: EVERYONE COMMITS TO THE MAIN

In trunk-based development, there's only one long-lived branch: the trunk. Everything happens there. All commits land there. All deployments ship from there.

Feature branches? If used, they're short-lived, hours, not days. Ideally, you're committing directly to the main branch behind a feature toggle (we'll discuss those in Chapter 4).

The mindset shift is radical, yet deceptively simple: **the codebase must always be shippable.** Not eventually. Not when QA says so. Now. At this very moment.

You wouldn't fly an aircraft that only occasionally works mid-flight. Why should your production code be different?

BUT WHAT ABOUT...?

Yes, yes. This is where the peanut gallery raises concerns.

"What about broken features?"

"What about unfinished work?"

"What if someone merges a bug?"

You handle all of that **in place**, not off to the side.

You **feature toggle** work that's not ready. You **write tests** to prevent regressions. You **automate pipelines** to catch issues before they land.

What you don't do is hide work in a cave for a month and then emerge blinking into the sunlight, asking for a code review the size of War and Peace.

VELOCITY WITHOUT THE WOBBLE

Trunk-based development isn't about speed for the sake of speed. It's about **velocity with stability**.

When everyone works on the same branch:

- You get immediate integration
- You reduce surprise bugs
- You kill the merge hell before it starts

Conflicts are shallow, fast, and visible. You're forced to communicate, test early, and think holistically. Your CI pipeline becomes a heartbeat, not a roulette wheel.

THE MOST COMMON EXCUSE: "BUT WE'RE NOT THAT MATURE YET"

Ironically, that's precisely why you need trunk-based development. Teams that wait to "get better" before embracing it rarely do. Why? Because branching enables procrastination. It allows technical debt to ferment in the shadows.

The truth is: **trunk-based development is what makes teams mature.** Not the other way around.

THE TACTICAL PLAYBOOK

Here's what to implement immediately:

- **Kill long-lived branches.** A good start is to ensure that no feature branch lives longer than 24 hours.
- **Enforce commit discipline.** Lint, type-check, and test every commit. No exceptions.
- **Use feature toggles.** Every significant new feature should be toggleable from Day 1.
- **Deploy from main.** Not from "release branches." Not from staging forks. Always from the main.

Bonus points:

- Tag each successful deploy.
- Automate rollback to the last green tag.
- Run your own code in staging *before* merging to main.

FINAL THOUGHT: THIS IS HOW ACCOUNTABLE TEAMS SHIP SOFTWARE

You wouldn't duct tape a parachute and hope for the best. Don't do it with your codebase either.

Trunk-based development isn't just a branching strategy; it's a development approach. It's a quiet standard of trust and technical maturity. That you trust your code, your process, and your engineers.

You're not "being agile."

You're just getting on with it.

CHAPTER 2
NO QA WALL
DEVELOPERS OWN QUALITY

Let's rip the bandage off early: **Your testers aren't the problem.** The wall between them and the developers is.

In the traditional tech org, testing is often treated like the digital equivalent of dishwashing. Developers create the meal; QA does the cleanup. It's a division of labour that makes intuitive sense — and that's precisely why it's so dangerous.

In modern SaaS, this wall doesn't just slow you down.

It breaks trust.

It breaks ownership.

And eventually, it breaks the product.

THE QUIET DEATH OF MANUAL TESTING

There was a time when manual testing made sense. GUIs were brittle, tooling was poor, and developers had neither the time nor patience to click through twelve modals before approving a checkout flow.

But it's 2025. Test automation tools are robust, fast, and integrate with your CI. E2E tests run in containers. Browsers simulate mobile gestures. You can fake a location in São Paulo and test your payment gateway without leaving your chair.

What remains of "manual QA" is usually one of two things:

1. **Regression babysitting.** (i.e., clicking around hoping nothing breaks)

2. **User simulation theatre.** (i.e., "Can you try logging in as a user from 2018 with a deactivated coupon?")

Let's be honest: these aren't high-leverage activities. They're repetitive, delay-prone, and completely solvable through automation — assuming developers take ownership.

THE MYTH OF THE QUALITY GATE

Traditional orgs imagine a pipeline like this:

`DEV --> QA --> UAT --> PROD`

Each arrow represents not just time but **distance** — distance from reality, from accountability, and from the customer. Bugs aren't fixed; they're "thrown back." Releases aren't fast; they're "pending validation." And when something breaks in production? It's a long game of Clue, except the murder weapon is always a spreadsheet.

Now imagine this instead:

`DEV --> PROD` (with tests, logs, and metrics)

That's not a shortcut. That's the real game.

QUALITY = DESIGN, NOT DETECTION

The dirty secret of testing is this: **quality is baked in, not inspected in.**

A well-tested system:

- Crashes loudly in CI, not silently in prod
- Has meaningful logs and alerts (written by the same people who wrote the code)
- Fails with dignity and observability

A poorly tested one?

- Passes QA on Tuesday
- Crashes for 2,000 users on Wednesday
- Triggers a war room on Thursday

And here's the kicker: the difference often lies not in testing volume, but in **developer mindset**.

When developers expect someone else to "catch the bugs," they optimise for velocity, not clarity. They push responsibility downstream. They view test failures as annoyances, rather than insights.

When developers **own quality**, everything shifts:

• They write better tests

• They log more deliberately

• They design for failure, not just success

EXPLORATORY TESTING? STILL VALUABLE. JUST NOT YOURS.

Now, before someone prints this chapter out and lights it on fire:

Exploratory testing **is** valuable. But not as a default, and not as a bottleneck.

It should be:

- **Rare** (reserved for risky or deeply human-centric features)
- **Targeted** (performed by product-minded engineers or designers)
- **Optional** (never on the critical path to release)

And even then, it's not about pass/fail — it's about insights. Behaviour, flow, fit. Things no CI suite can fully capture.

The QA role of the future isn't a bug-hunter. It's a **quality coach**. A person who builds frameworks, guides test strategy, and helps teams understand risk. Think of them less like inspectors and more like flight instructors.

WHAT HAPPENS WHEN DEVELOPERS TEST THEIR OWN CODE

Now we come to the point that may seem heretical to some: **developers testing their own code is not a conflict of interest. It's a duty.**

Yes, they'll miss things. Yes, they'll be biased. But they'll also:

- Catch bugs earlier (because feedback loops are shorter)
- Understand the system better (because tests force them to)
- Build safer systems (because no one wants to wake up at 3:00 a.m.)

If your team has a culture of blame, this won't work. But if your team has a culture of **accountability**, it will thrive.

Because here's the truth: the best way to improve quality is to stop outsourcing it.

TACTICAL IMPLEMENTATION

Here's what you do this quarter:

- **Shift testing left.** Tests run in CI. Not in QA.
- **Kill manual regression testing.** Replace with automated suites. Always.
- **Make every developer responsible for writing tests.** Unit, integration, and E2E.
- **Give developers access to logs and alert dashboards.** If they break it, they see it first.
- **Invest in test infrastructure engineers.** These are the multipliers — build tools, not barriers.

Optional but highly effective:

- Set a rule: **No untested code is ever merged.**
- Create a "Testing Playbook" tailored to your stack and system.
- Run *pre-mortems* instead of test plans: "How could this fail?"

FINAL THOUGHT: QUALITY IS EVERYONE'S PROBLEM — BUT IT STARTS WITH DEVS

If you're still hiring a QA team to guard the gates, you're solving yesterday's problem.

The modern SaaS product changes ten times a day. If testing is a separate phase, you're always too late.

The best testing strategy is simple:

- **Write tests.**
- **Run them in CI.**
- **Fix what breaks.**
- **Deploy when green.**

Anything more is decoration.

CHAPTER 3
CONTINUOUS DELIVERY
NOT "CI/CD" THEATRE

For many teams, "CI/CD" is a checkbox rather than a capability. They point to their Jenkins dashboard, their GitHub Actions config, or their "green" pipeline and say, "See? We've got CI/CD." But ask how often they deploy to production, and the answer is either "once a week" or "well... it depends."

Let's be clear. Continuous Delivery isn't about tools. It's about behaviour. It means your software is always in a deployable state — every commit, every day. If shipping to production requires a Slack thread, a manual approval, or lighting a ceremonial candle, then you don't have CD. You have a ceremony, not a system.

WHAT CD REALLY MEANS

Continuous Delivery is simple in principle:

Every change that passes automated tests should be *immediately deployable* to production.

Note: "Deployable" doesn't mean it must go live to users. That's where toggles and controls come in. What matters is that the pipeline can deliver it safely, consistently, and without fear. If you have to stop and think, "Is it safe to deploy right now?" — then your system isn't ready. You're not practising CD. You're still negotiating with your own stack.

SIGNS YOU'RE DOING CD PROPERLY

A real CD system has certain characteristics that go beyond just running builds and tests. You'll notice:

- **Frequent production deployments**: daily at minimum, ideally multiple times per day.

- **No separate "release" phase**: deployment *is* the release mechanism.
- **Zero reliance on manual QA**: automated testing gates the pipeline.
- **Confident Friday deploys**: because the rollback path is clear and tested.
- **No ticket shuffling**: shipping is part of the commit workflow, not a separate project.

CD makes releasing code feel as routine as saving a file. That's the goal: flow without drama.

WHY MOST TEAMS FAKE IT

Plenty of teams claim CI/CD but still have deployments that:

- Require multiple sign-offs
- Only happens on Wednesdays
- Are driven by Jira status, not system state
- Break more than they fix

Here's what's often happening behind the scenes:

DEV → COMMIT

↓

Run some tests (if Jenkins feels like it)

↓

Wait for QA sign-off

↓

Push to staging

↓

Test again manually

↓

Open a ticket for ops

↓

Deploy when someone approves

↓

Pray

. . .

This is not continuous. It's a cautious waterfall with YAML in the middle.

WHAT A REAL CD PIPELINE LOOKS LIKE

Let's contrast that with a working CD pipeline. A healthy one looks like this:

1. **Commit to main.** All changes flow through the trunk. No long-lived branches.
2. **Automated checks trigger.** Linting, unit tests, integration tests, and static analysis.
3. **Build and artefact generation.** Reproducible, tagged, and versioned.
4. **Deploy to staging automatically**. Uses the same pipeline as production.
5. **Run smoke tests.** Basic validation of key functionality.
6. **Promote to production.** Can be immediate, cohort-based, or toggle-driven.
7. **Monitor, alert, and rollback if needed**. Telemetry is in place and real-time.

This is what "continuous" actually looks like: *no human bottlenecks, no forks, no drama.*

GETTING THERE: CD FUNDAMENTALS

You don't need perfection from day one, but you do need the right foundations. To practice real CD:

- **Deploy from the main** branch, not from staging forks or release branches.
- **Make tests meaningful and fast**: brittle tests slow everything down and erode trust.
- **Automate everything**: builds, deploys, environment setup, rollbacks.
- **Eliminate handoffs**: especially between dev, QA, and ops.
- **Build rollback paths** using versioned artefacts, blue-green deployments, or feature toggles.

And most importantly: **deploy often**. The more you ship, the less scary each deploy becomes.

WATCH OUT FOR THESE RED FLAGS

Even teams with good intentions fall into old traps. If you see these patterns, your CD system is probably not what you think it is:

- **"We deploy every sprint."** That's just scheduled batch releases.
- **Manual approvals in the pipeline.** If a human can block a deploy, it's not continuous.
- **"We wait for QA."** Quality should be validated in CI.
- **Separate deploy pipelines for staging and prod.** Your systems should mirror each other.

The most telling sign? If deployments are stressful, you haven't finished the job.

CULTURAL SHIFT: MAKE DEPLOYMENTS BORING

Ultimately, CD is a cultural practice as much as it is a technical one. It requires teams to stop viewing deployment as a high-risk event and start treating it as part of everyday work.

When deploys are boring:

- You deploy more often.
- Each change is smaller and safer.
- You catch problems early.
- You build trust across the team.

That trust lets you move faster *and* sleep better.

FINAL THOUGHT: IT'S NOT ABOUT TOOLS — IT'S ABOUT CONFIDENCE

A CI/CD pipeline isn't impressive because it runs. It's impressive because you trust it. Trust is built on simplicity, consistency, and discipline.

If you still need to ask, "Is it safe to deploy?" — the answer is no.

Real Continuous Delivery doesn't ask. It just works.

CHAPTER 4
FEATURE TOGGLES
THE ART OF CONTROLLED CHAOS

Feature toggles are one of the most powerful tools in modern software engineering — and also among the most misunderstood.

Used well, they allow teams to ship incomplete features, test in production, run experiments, and decouple deployment from release. Used poorly, they create technical debt, cognitive overhead, and haunted code paths that haven't been toggled on since 2021.

But at their core, toggles are simple. They let you deploy code without exposing it.

In other words, **they're the control system for your chaos**.

WHY FEATURE TOGGLES MATTER

Let's say you've adopted trunk-based development. Everyone is committing to the main, every day. Excellent. However, not every feature is ready to be seen by users, and not every experiment should be deployed to production all at once. You want control without slowing the flow.

That's where toggles shine. They give you the ability to:

- **Deploy incomplete work safely** without waiting for full functionality.
- **Gradually roll out** features to cohorts, markets, or device types.
- **Run A/B or multivariate experiments** in production environments.
- **Quickly disable failing features** without triggering a rollback.

Without toggles, your only options are branching (which slows you down) or hoping your incomplete feature doesn't explode in prod (which is not recommended).

TYPES OF TOGGLES (AND WHEN TO USE THEM)

Not all toggles are created equal. Understanding the types helps you use them intentionally and avoid toggle debt.

- **Release Toggles.** Used to hide incomplete features in production. These are short-lived and should be deleted once the feature is fully rolled out.
- **Experiment Toggles.** Used for A/B testing or gradual rollouts. These often integrate with analytics and can live longer, but should be monitored closely.
- **Ops Toggles.** Used to disable expensive or risky features during outages or heavy loads. These should be easily flipped via the dashboard or API.
- **Permission Toggles.** Used to manage feature access per user role or tier. These are often long-lived and require careful governance.

Key advice: Tag your toggles clearly by type. What lives long should be documented. What lives short should be deleted ruthlessly.

ANTI-PATTERNS TO AVOID

With great toggling power comes great toggling responsibility. The benefits evaporate quickly if you fall into these traps:

- **Leaving toggles in forever** – Forgotten toggles turn into dead branches in the tree. Remove them as soon as the feature is fully launched.
- **Toggle logic everywhere** – Don't sprinkle if feature_enabled across dozens of files. Use centralised wrappers or gates.
- **Nested toggles** – Two toggles dependent on each other lead to Schrödinger's feature. If the logic diagram needs a whiteboard, it's already too complex.
- **No toggle registry** – If you don't know what toggles exist or who owns them, you're not managing your system. You're babysitting it.

HOW TO DO TOGGLES WELL

A sound toggle system is clean, documented, and operationally safe. You should aim for:

- **Centralised management**
  - Utilise platforms like LaunchDarkly, Unleash, or create your own custom dashboards.
  - Visibility across all active toggles, current states, and owners.
- **Toggles as configuration**
  - Controlled via API, DB, or config files, not hardcoded.

    - Flippable in real time, not just at deploy.
- **Auditable toggles**
    - Track who toggled what, when, and why.
    - Ideal for incident reviews and feature accountability.
- **Integration with monitoring**
    - If a toggle causes errors, alerts should spike accordingly.
    - Good systems allow you to track performance per toggle state.

Bonus principle: Pair every toggle with an expiration date or condition. "Remove when 100% of users have feature X" should be visible from day one.

THE LIFECYCLE OF A FEATURE FLAG

To keep toggles manageable, follow a deliberate lifecycle:

1. **Create the toggle** with a clear name, purpose, and owner.
2. **Deploy the feature behind the toggle** to production, but leave it off.
3. **Test and validate** in staging or with internal users.
4. **Gradually enable** via cohort, region, or percentage.
5. **Monitor closely** for errors, load, and user behaviour.
6. **Flip entirely on** once confidence is high.
7. **Delete the toggle** and clean up associated logic.

Toggles are not stickers, they're levers. Use them, then remove them.

REAL-WORLD USE: CONTROLLED CHAOS IN ACTION

One high-growth SaaS company I worked with used toggles not only to launch features but to defuse incidents. They had a toggle for their recommendation engine, which, like many machine-learning features, occasionally lost its mind and recommended absolute nonsense. When the alerts started coming in, they simply flipped the toggle off. No rollback. No redeploy. Just... control.

That's the magic: deploying every day, experimenting in prod, and still having your hand on the wheel.

FINAL THOUGHT: FEARLESS DELIVERY REQUIRES CONTROL

Fast deploys without toggles are reckless.

Toggles without cleanup decay.

What you want is that rare middle ground: the ability to deliver constantly, adapt quickly, and roll back cleanly — all without touching your deployment system.

Feature toggles give you that power. Just don't mistake power for permission to be messy.

Use them deliberately. Track them carefully. Retire them often.

They're not your safety net.

They're your steering wheel.

CHAPTER 5

TESTING THAT ACTUALLY WORKS

In most teams, testing is a mix of hope and habit. Some tests catch bugs. Some slow things down. A few are flaky enough to warrant their own incident channel.

But for all the talk of quality, few teams have a coherent testing strategy. They either overtest, undertest, or run everything everywhere until something passes. At worst, testing becomes performance art — designed to impress auditors, not protect users.

Let's reset the table.

Testing isn't about coverage. It's about confidence.

The right test suite makes deployment feel safe. The wrong one creates noise, slows delivery, and breeds distrust.

WHAT REAL-WORLD TESTING ACTUALLY LOOKS LIKE

There's no one-size-fits-all pyramid, but there are clear roles for each test type. Think of it not as a hierarchy, but a toolkit, with each layer doing a specific job.

1. Unit Tests

The foundation. Fast, focused, and fiercely local.

- Test a single function or method in isolation.
- Should run in milliseconds.
- Pure logic, no external dependencies.

Use these to:

- Validate edge cases.
- Lock down expected behaviour.
- Act as executable documentation.

2. Integration Tests

Test components *together*, not apart.

- Validate real-world interactions: DBs, queues, APIs.
- Slower than unit tests but far more informative.
- Crucial for identifying system drift.

Focus these on:

- Service-to-service contracts.
- State transitions (e.g., user signup flows).
- Data persistence and side effects.

3. Contract Tests

Especially critical in microservices or third-party integrations.

- Validate *agreements* between services.
- Don't test logic — test *expectations.*
- Help catch breaking changes before they ship.

These are most useful when:

- You own both sides of the contract (and want version safety).
- You're working with external APIs that change frequently.

4. End-to-End (E2E) Tests

The most misunderstood layer.

- Simulate real user actions through the UI or API.
- Run in staging or ephemeral environments.
- Slowest and most brittle, use sparingly.

E2E tests should:

- Cover core paths only: login, checkout, and onboarding.
- Be stable, headless, and independent.

- Fail fast and report clearly.

If your test suite has more E2E tests than unit tests, something's off.

ANTI-PATTERNS THAT BREAK TEAMS

You've likely seen at least one of these in the wild:

- **Flaky tests accepted as normal.** Teams rerun failed builds until something passes. Confidence erodes. Discipline dies.
- **E2E bloat.** Every new feature gets a Selenium test. Eventually, deployments grind to a halt.
- **Over-mocking**. Unit tests become so isolated that they lose value. You're testing mocks, not behaviour.
- **"100% coverage" worship.** This doesn't mean quality, it often means busywork.
- **Manual test phases.** If it can be tested manually, it can be automated (and probably should be).

WHAT HIGH-CONFIDENCE TESTING LOOKS LIKE

Great testing feels like this:

- Developers trust failures. A red test is a real problem.
- Tests are fast. Unit and integration tests run in minutes, not hours.
- The test suite is a gate, not a formality.
- There's no manual test plan. It's codified, repeatable, and versioned.
- Test failures block merges, without escalation.

You're not writing tests to impress compliance. You're writing tests because you hate surprises.

BUILDING THE RIGHT CULTURE AROUND TESTING

Tools matter, but testing is first a **cultural discipline**. The best teams:

- **Write tests before or during implementation.** Especially integration and contract tests. They help clarify design.
- **Review tests like production code.** No one should create a 500-line test file that no one else can understand.
- **Treat test quality as system quality.** Bad tests are bugs, they deserve just as much urgency.

- **Continuously prune the test suite.** Remove outdated tests. Clean up redundancy. Refactor where needed.

Also, if a test fails often but no one fixes it, delete it. It's doing more harm than good.

Tactical Implementation: How to Fix Your Tests in 30 Days

Week 1:

- Audit all flaky tests.
- Tag and isolate them. Make them optional (temporarily).
- Set a rule: no new code without tests.

Week 2:

- Rebuild a clean CI layer: run fast unit tests first, then integration tests, and finally, optional E2E tests.
- Start writing contract tests between critical services.

Week 3:

- Refactor the existing E2E suite to test only primary flows.
- Automate smoke tests post-deploy.

Week 4:

- Add visual dashboards: what passed, what failed, and why.
- Introduce test metrics: flake rate, runtime, and failure recovery speed.

Then: **maintain**. Testing isn't a one-time fix. It's a long-term hygiene habit.

FINAL THOUGHT: TEST LIKE YOU'RE ON CALL

Write the kind of tests you'd want if you were responsible for a 2:00 a.m. incident.

Because, eventually, you will be.

Tests are your early warning system. Done right, they'll save your night. Done wrong, they'll ruin your week.

CHAPTER 6
PIPELINES THAT HEAL THEMSELVES

You can tell a lot about a team by watching how they respond to a broken pipeline. Some shrug it off. Some panic. Some fix it immediately. And some (unfortunately, the majority) work around it quietly, like slipping past a sleeping guard. Over time, broken pipelines stop being exceptions. They become the background noise.

Here's the problem:

A pipeline you don't trust is a pipeline you don't use.

And when that happens, everything downstream begins to rot.

Modern SaaS delivery requires pipelines that are not just functional but resilient. They don't just move code, they guide decisions. If your pipeline lies, stalls, or throws tantrums, it becomes an obstacle. But when it works reliably, it becomes a source of confidence. You ship faster, safer, and with less second-guessing.

WHAT A HEALTHY PIPELINE FEELS LIKE

In a well-functioning pipeline:

- Commits flow through in minutes, not hours.
- Failures are clear, actionable, and accurate.
- Developers believe red builds indicate real issues.
- No one fears the deploy button.

The experience should be **predictable and boring**. If you push code on a Friday, the system should behave no differently than it did on Tuesday. That's what reliability looks like.

BUT MOST PIPELINES ARE NOT HEALTHY

Many pipelines start with good intentions, but slowly drift into dysfunction. Typical symptoms include:

- **Flaky tests** causing red builds without real failures.
- **Slow feedback loops**: developers wait 30+ minutes to find out if their code broke something.
- **Silent failures**: a deploy succeeds, but the monitoring never ran.
- **Spaghetti logic** in YAML or scripted pipelines: fragile, hard to debug, and known only to one DevOps engineer.

Eventually, teams stop trusting the pipeline. They run things locally. They rerun failing jobs, hoping for green. And they revert to tribal knowledge: "Ask Maria before you merge, she knows how to get it through."

At that point, your pipeline is no longer a tool. It's a gatekeeper. A broken one.

WHAT MAKES A PIPELINE SELF-HEALING?

You can't eliminate all flakiness, but you can **design for recovery**. A self-healing pipeline doesn't mean infallibility, it implies *robustness*. The ability to detect, isolate, and recover from routine failure.

Key features of a self-healing pipeline:

- **Flake detection and quarantine.** Flaky tests are automatically flagged and rerun in isolation. Persistent offenders are logged and scheduled for review.
- **Retry logic for transient failures.** Network hiccups, race conditions, or rate limits shouldn't break a build.
- **Pipeline observability.** Metrics on success rate, runtime, flake rate, and test coverage are visible to the team. Logs are readable and traceable per step.
- **Fail-fast logic.** Don't waste 20 minutes running tests if the build failed at step 2. Dependencies are checked early and loudly.
- **Parallelisation and caching.** Speed up test runs without cutting corners. Cache dependencies, shard test jobs.
- **Slack (or chat) integration.** Notifications include logs, status, and rerun options, not just "Build failed."

When pipelines self-correct or isolate issues, teams stop fearing them. And that changes everything.

HOW TO BUILD IT: PRACTICAL STEPS

Start by auditing what you have. Ask:

- What's our average build time?
- What's our flake rate?
- How long does it take to recover from a red build?
- How often do we bypass or ignore the pipeline?

Then, improve iteratively:

1. **Tag and isolate flaky tests.** Add @flake tags or equivalent markers. Treat them like real bugs.
2. **Add retry logic to the pipeline.** Especially for test setup steps or infrastructure provisioning.
3. **Introduce a flake quarantine system.** When a test fails inconsistently, automatically move it to a separate pipeline path and notify the team.
4. **Enable fast feedback.** Run linters, type checks, and unit tests in parallel. Delay slow tests until after early gates pass.
5. **Use dashboards, not black boxes.** Make the test and deploy status visible. Track trends. Let the team know what's improving and what isn't.
6. **Codify health rules.** For example: "Any pipeline with >10% flake rate is frozen until resolved." Make it policy, not a suggestion.

ENGINEERING FOR VELOCITY REQUIRES ENGINEERING FOR STABILITY

Speed doesn't come from brute force. It comes from **removing friction**. And broken pipelines are pure friction: invisible at first, then constant.

In high-performing SaaS orgs, developers trust the pipeline to catch mistakes, provide feedback, and guide deployment decisions. In lower-performing ones, the pipeline is viewed like an old elevator: use at your own risk.

The good news? Fixing pipelines is high-leverage work. It pays off quickly and visibly.

FINAL THOUGHT: A PIPELINE IS A MIRROR

Your pipeline reflects how your team thinks about quality.

If it's slow, brittle, and noisy, your team will be slow, brittle, and noisy.

If it's clean, trustworthy, and fast, your team will ship with confidence.

Make it heal.

Make it honest.

Make it boring.

CHAPTER 7
IMMUTABLE INFRASTRUCTURE AND INFRA-AS-CODE

Shipping code is only half the story. The other half, the part that most teams underestimate until it blows up, is the environment in which code runs. How it's built, deployed, configured, and scaled.

For many SaaS teams, environments are treated like family kitchens. There's a general layout, but everyone has their own way of doing things. Some configs live in shell scripts. Others are whispered tribal knowledge. The production box is "special." And if something breaks, you SSH in and patch it live, then swear you'll clean it up later.

That was tolerable in 2009. In 2025, it's malpractice.

WHAT IS IMMUTABLE INFRASTRUCTURE?

In short: you **don't modify running systems**. You replace them.

Rather than logging into a server and updating packages, you build a new, clean version with the change already baked in. That version is tested, tagged, and deployed, and then the old one is decommissioned.

This approach means:

- **No drift.** Every instance is identical, every time.
- **Repeatability.** Dev, staging, and prod match.
- **Confidence.** If it worked in staging, it'll work in prod, because they're the same artefact.

Think of your infrastructure like deploying a container, not renovating a house.

WHY "SSH-ING INTO PROD" MUST DIE

The moment you allow live access to infrastructure, you allow untracked changes, inconsistent environments, and late-night heroics. It feels fast in the moment, like slapping duct tape on a leak. But over time, that chaos accumulates.

Live edits:

- Aren't version-controlled
- Can't be rolled back easily
- Encourage undocumented "fixes"
- Undermine trust in every deploy

Instead, all infrastructure changes should be made **in code**, reviewed like any other pull request, and deployed like any other change.

ENTER INFRASTRUCTURE AS CODE (IAC)

Infra-as-Code means your infrastructure lives in your repository. It's versioned, peer-reviewed, and testable. It replaces "runbook" culture with clarity.

Popular tools:

- **Terraform**: declarative, cross-cloud, and mature.
- **Pulumi**: similar, but lets you write infra in TypeScript, Python, etc.
- **Ansible**: better suited for configuration than provisioning.
- **CloudFormation**: AWS-native, robust but verbose.

With IaC:

- You can recreate your entire environment with one command.
- You can destroy and rebuild staging daily (or even hourly).
- You can trace every change in a git log, including who made it and why.

In other words, infra stops being magic. It becomes **predictable engineering**.

HOW TO ADOPT IT (WITHOUT CREATING A MESS)

If your team is still doing infrastructure manually, don't try to terraform the moon on day one. Start incrementally:

1. **Select one environment** (typically staging) and document the setup.

2. **Track changes in git**: no more one-off changes through the console.
3. **Run a destroy → rebuild cycle weekly** to force drift detection.
4. **Use modules** to abstract common patterns (e.g., database + monitoring).
5. **Add a CI job** to validate infrastructure changes before the merge.
6. **Use remote state management** (e.g., S3 + DynamoDB lock for Terraform) to prevent team collisions.

Most importantly: ban undocumented console changes. No ticket, no merge, no push — no change.

IMMUTABLE DEPLOYMENTS IN PRACTICE

True immutability means that when you deploy a new version of your app:

- A **new container** or VM is created.
- It runs side by side with the old one (blue-green or rolling).
- Once verified, the old one is shut down or discarded.

There are no hotfixes. No SSH. No, "just tweak that config real quick." Everything flows through the pipeline.

This enables:

- **Faster rollbacks**: just redeploy the previous artefact.
- **Consistent auditing**: every deploy has a fingerprint.
- **Safety under stress**: in an incident, you don't fix prod; you replace it.

And yes, this works. Every high-scale SaaS org you admire is doing precisely this.

THE COST OF NOT DOING IT

If your team still:

- Has hand-built servers that "just work"
- Treats staging like a suggestion
- Has no idea what changed between deploys
- Schedules downtime windows "just in case"...

...then you're flying without instruments.

These aren't minor issues. They are fundamental liabilities. And they only get worse as you grow.

FINAL THOUGHT: ENVIRONMENTS SHOULD BE BORING

You should never be afraid to destroy and recreate an environment.

You should never patch anything manually in production.

You should never have to say, "It worked on staging, but prod is... different."

Infrastructure should be invisible, versioned, disposable, and boring.

Make it so.

CHAPTER 8
DEPLOYMENTS SHOULD BE FREQUENT
AND BORING

There's a peculiar habit in software teams: they treat deployments like weddings.

Big ceremony. Lots of planning. Nervous participants. And someone always cries.

But unlike weddings, deployments should happen all the time. Quietly. Without stress. Without drama. Just another part of the day.

In a healthy SaaS environment, **deployments are ordinary**. They occur frequently, often without fanfare, and fear. This isn't about carelessness, it's about competence. Confidence. Control. The ability to ship whenever needed, because your system and your team are ready.

WHY FREQUENCY IS SAFETY

Deploying more often doesn't increase risk — it **reduces it**.

Here's why:

- **Smaller changes** are easier to test, debug, and reason about.
- **Faster feedback** means bugs are caught sooner.
- **Rollbacks are cleaner** because you always know what changed.
- **Incidents are shorter** since root causes are narrow in scope.

Conversely, large deployments are dangerous. The more you pack into a release, the harder it is to validate. Every dependency, every feature, every migration becomes part of a tangled knot. One failure can cascade across multiple systems, and the rollback often feels like trying to put toothpaste back into the tube.

Small, frequent deploys act like pressure valves. They prevent buildup — and therefore prevent explosions.

THE ANATOMY OF A BORING DEPLOY

Boring doesn't mean careless. Boring means **smooth**. You want deploys to become muscle memory: a practised, controlled movement, not a leap of faith.

A boring deployment looks like this:

1. **Trigger.** CI passes. Code merges to main. The deployment pipeline kicks off.
2. **Build.** Artefact is built, tested, and versioned.
3. **Deploy to staging.** Identical to production. Smoke tests run.
4. **Deploy to production.** Toggle is off by default. Canary rollout or full launch.
5. **Observe.** Alerts, metrics, logs — all green. Toggle on.
6. **Move on.** No war room. No celebration. No dread.

This is routine. It's not a launch. It's just the next step.

GOOD TEAMS DEPLOY FREQUENTLY. GREAT TEAMS DEPLOY WITHOUT FLINCHING.

It's common to hear, "We deploy once a week." Sometimes, once a sprint. Rarely, daily.

Here's the harsh truth:

If you can't deploy at will, you're not ready to scale.

The goal isn't just frequency for frequency's sake. It's **flexibility**:

- Can you deploy on Friday?
- Can you deploy during a marketing campaign?
- Can you hotfix without panicking?
- Can you roll back with one command?

If the answer is no, your delivery process is fragile.

Great teams build systems where **deployment isn't a special event**, it's the default state.

KILL THE FEAR. BUILD THE SYSTEM.

If your team fears deployment, the solution isn't to deploy less. The solution is to **fix the reasons they're scary**.

Common fears, and how to eliminate them:

- *"Deploys break things."* Add tests, enforce pipeline health, and practice rollbacks.
- *"We can't rollback cleanly."* Use versioned artefacts, blue-green deployments, or toggles.
- *"We need QA to sign off."* Automate test gates. Shift testing left.
- *"Staging doesn't match prod."* Use immutable infrastructure. Codify everything.
- *"The last deploy was a mess."* Do smaller, more frequent ones to reduce scope and risk.

Deployments don't become boring on their own. You make them boring by building safety into the system.

DEPLOY LOGS ARE A REFLECTION OF TEAM MATURITY

One of the most revealing artefacts in a SaaS company is the deployment log.

If it's full of skipped deploys, panic threads, hotfixes, and finger-pointing, then the team is reacting, not delivering. If it's full of calm, timestamped entries with successful outcomes, quiet toggles, and no surprises… then you're on the right track.

Calm deploys suggest a calm culture. A team that understands how to build safely, and knows when to pause, but rarely needs to.

WHEN TO DEPLOY

If your system supports it, there's no wrong time. But there are good *habits*:

- Deploy **in the morning**: gives you the whole day to react if needed.
- Avoid **deploying before major holidays**: not because it's scary, but because no one wants to babysit a system from a ski lodge.
- Prefer **automated deploys on merge**: especially when behind toggles.
- Be ready to **deploy on demand**: for fixes, fast follow-ups, and experiments.

The only bad habit? **Hoarding changes** and releasing them all at once. That's not delivery. That's gambling.

FINAL THOUGHT: DEPLOY LIKE IT'S TUESDAY

Deploying should feel like brushing your teeth: routine, unremarkable, and not worth tweeting about.

If your deployments are stressful, fix the system.

If they're rare, reduce your batch size.

If they're noisy, make them boring.

Because when your deployments are boring, your product can be exciting.

CHAPTER 9
OBSERVABILITY IS A SHARED LANGUAGE

In high-functioning teams, observability isn't tacked on at the end — it's part of the conversation from the very first commit. It isn't a checkbox for compliance or a dashboard to impress investors. It's the language your system uses to speak, and the tool your team uses to understand what it's saying.

Modern SaaS systems are fast, distributed, and complex. By the time a user notices something is broken, the problem has already mutated across services. You can't debug what you can't see. You can't trust what you can't explain. And you certainly can't scale what you can't measure.

So let's establish a simple truth:

Observability is not an ops function. It's a team-wide discipline.

WHAT OBSERVABILITY ACTUALLY IS

Too many teams confuse observability with "monitoring," or worse, with "we have logs."

Observability is the ability to **understand what your system is doing internally based on its external outputs**. It allows you to answer questions you didn't anticipate asking.

It isn't just data collection, it's a design choice. An intentional structuring of how your software narrates its behaviour through:

- **Logs**: detailed records of events and state changes.
- **Metrics**: numerical aggregates like latency, request count, or error rate.
- **Traces**: end-to-end journey of a single request across systems.

Together, they give you context. Not just what broke, but how and why.

THE FOUR GOLDEN SIGNALS

At a minimum, every system (and ideally every central feature) should track these four signals, known as Google's "Golden Signals":

- **Latency:** How long does a request take?
- **Traffic:** How many requests are we handling?
- **Errors:** How many of them are failing?
- **Saturation:** How close are we to our resource limits?

These should not be abstract numbers buried in a dashboard. They should be visible, owned, and used to trigger discussion when something changes.

If you only have time to do one thing well, focus on monitoring **latency under load**. It exposes both performance issues and downstream instability faster than any other signal.

DEVELOPERS OWN THE TELEMETRY

The era of devs throwing code over the wall and ops "keeping the lights on" is over. In 2025, developers write the logs, define the metrics, and configure the alerts, because they are closest to the code and most capable of identifying what matters.

That means:

- Writing structured logs, not `printlns` or vague strings.
- Emitting custom metrics per feature or endpoint.
- Setting thresholds and alert logic as part of the feature, rather than afterwards.
- Reviewing telemetry as part of the pull request, not the postmortem.

If you wrote the feature, you should know how to tell when it's working and when it's not.

CHARACTERISTICS OF HEALTHY OBSERVABILITY

A well-instrumented system doesn't shout, it informs. The signal is clean, the feedback is fast, and the team trusts what they see.

Here's what that looks like in practice:

- **Logs** are structured (in JSON or a similar format) and consistently formatted, including correlation and request IDs.
- **Metrics** are visible in real-time and tied to features, not just infrastructure.
- **Traces** map the flow of a user request across services, highlighting where time is spent or failures occur.

- **Dashboards** are actively used, not just decorative.
- **Alerts** are actionable, rare, and owned — no one's drowning in noise.

A single deployment should leave a **coherent and contextual telemetry fingerprint**: logs, metrics, and traces. This isn't overhead. It's confidence.

SMELLS OF POOR OBSERVABILITY

You don't need a PhD in SRE to spot bad observability. It usually looks like this:

- "Let's add more logs and redeploy" as a first response.
- Alerts that fire at 2:00 a.m. with no actionable information.
- Dashboards with stale or duplicated panels.
- Metrics named inconsistently or worse, not named at all.
- Logging so verbose that real issues are buried in noise.

Another red flag: developers who don't know how to check their own feature in production. If you can't trace what you've built, you can't support it.

MAKING OBSERVABILITY A FIRST-CLASS PRACTICE

To build the right culture around observability, integrate it into the same workflows as code, tests, and deploys.

- **Code reviews include telemetry.** If a feature has user impact, it should emit something.
- **Dashboards are version-controlled.** Use dashboard-as-code when possible (e.g., Grafana JSON or Terraform modules).
- **Every service has a visibility contract.** What it emits, what it expects, and how it fails.
- **On-call teams own alerts.** No "info only" pings. Every alert should be tied to a specific action or decision.

This creates alignment: devs build what they monitor. And what gets monitored improves.

BONUS PRACTICES FOR A STRONGER SIGNAL

If you've got the basics in place, take it up a notch:

- Use **correlation IDs** to track user sessions across microservices.
- Redact and rate-limit logs to minimise noise and prevent the exposure of sensitive data.
- Build **feature-level dashboards**, not just per-service ones. You want to know how your checkout flow is performing, not just how "service-X" is doing.

- Write **postmortems with telemetry graphs**. Don't just explain what went wrong, *show* it.
- Rotate dashboard ownership monthly: someone new owns it, updates it, and defends its usefulness.

The goal is to treat observability as a **dynamic interface**, not a static report. It evolves with your product.

FINAL THOUGHT: SYSTEMS SPEAK. YOU JUST NEED TO LISTEN.

Observability is empathy: technical empathy for your system, and for your users.

It's not about catching fires. It's about seeing the smoke before the spark.

It's about building a product that explains itself, so you can respond quickly, learn continuously, and ship confidently.

Don't just collect data.

Design your software to narrate its story — clearly, calmly, and in real time.

CHAPTER 10
YOU BUILD IT, YOU OWN IT

Let's start with something uncomfortable:

Your team doesn't need more QA engineers. It needs tighter feedback loops and people willing to take own them.

Because ownership — real, technical ownership — is the quiet, unglamorous backbone of every high-performing SaaS team. Not because it's trendy. Not because it earns praise. But because without it, everything else falls apart.

Ownership means that the same person who writes the code is also responsible for testing, shipping, monitoring, and responding when it misbehaves. It's the polar opposite of what many teams are still doing: spreading accountability so thin it becomes invisible.

In teams without clear ownership, production incidents often devolve into finger-pointing sessions. Postmortems sound like political campaigns. Bugs become orphans. And everyone is genuinely surprised when nothing is fixed.

But in teams that own their work, a different pattern emerges. Code is written with foresight. Alerts are meaningful. Rollbacks are clean. When something breaks, it's addressed with urgency, not ceremony. There's no escalation path, just responsibility.

WHAT OWNERSHIP ACTUALLY MEANS

Let's clear away the confusion. ownership is not a slogan. It's not a job title. It's not "caring a lot."

It's this:

- If you ship it, you test it. No one else is coming.
- If it breaks, you respond. No one else is on-call for your mistake.
- If the alert fires, you investigate. No one else wrote that log line.
- If the deployment fails, you fix the pipeline. No one else has the context.

This isn't a punishment. It's how real teams move fast without fear.

ON-CALL IS A FEATURE, NOT A BUG

Developers used to dread pager duty. Many still do. However, in a high-trust system, being on call isn't a punishment. It's the purest expression of technical respect.

You're trusted to ship to production; therefore, you're trusted to support production. You don't need to be an ops expert. But you need to know how to read your own logs. You need to know what "healthy" looks like for your service. And if you don't, you're not done.

When developers carry the pager, they build differently. They think through failure paths. They log better. They write tests that matter. Because they know: they'll be the ones waking up.

It's amazing how fast "why did this alert fire?" becomes "why didn't I catch this earlier?" — and how quickly that changes behaviour.

PLATFORM TEAMS ARE NOT YOUR SAFETY NET

One of the most persistent misunderstandings in modern orgs is the role of platform teams.

Good platform teams don't own your reliability. They don't babysit your pipeline. They're not a DevOps concierge.

They exist to:

- Provide paved roads: reusable CI/CD, infra modules, observability tooling.
- Standardise tooling, so you don't reinvent the wheel every sprint.
- Build golden paths, so delivery is safe, fast, and boring.

They do not:

- Debug your service.
- Write your tests.
- Own your deploys.

Platform teams are multipliers. But if you rely on them as crutches, all they do is mask weakness.

SYMPTOMS OF A NO-OWNERSHIP CULTURE

You can smell the lack of ownership before you see it. It sounds like this:

- "Let's wait for QA to confirm."
- "That's an ops issue."
- "Do we know who owns that service?"
- "I think someone changed something in prod…"

None of this is evil. But all of it is slow. And eventually, it breaks things in a way you can't duct-tape back together.

Ownership removes friction not by adding process, but by eliminating ambiguity. Everyone knows who to call. Better yet, they don't need to.

CULTURE DOESN'T CREATE OWNERSHIP — PRACTICE DOES

This part is critical. You don't inspire ownership with posters, town halls, or values decks. You enforce it by how the work is structured.

- Every service has an accountable owner.
- Every deploy is owned by the person who merged it.
- Every incident includes the person who introduced the change.
- Every alert has an assignee, not a shared inbox.
- Every postmortem leads to a change, not a meeting.

You don't need a framework. You need consistency. And a little courage.

FINAL THOUGHT: YOU WROTE IT. YOU RUN IT.

The most brilliant engineers don't build the best systems. The most accountable ones do.

Accountability doesn't mean perfection. You'll still miss things. You'll still break prod. But you'll do it with your eyes open — and your hands on the controls.

If you're not sure who owns a system, the answer is: no one.

And in software, that's where entropy begins.

So own it. Not because it's noble. But because it's faster. Cleaner. Quieter.

And in the long run, far less painful.

CHAPTER 11
METRICS THAT MATTER
FLOW, FAILURE, AND FEEDBACK

Most teams measure too much and learn too little.

Dashboards overflow with numbers: velocity, story points, "developer satisfaction," test counts, code churn. But ask a simple question — *Are we getting better?* — and the room goes quiet.

This is the core dysfunction of metrics in software teams: **when everything is measured, nothing is understood**.

The tragedy isn't that metrics are useless. It's that the right ones are so often drowned in noise.

Because the right metrics are rarely exciting, they're certainly not glamorous. But they are brutally revealing. They make people uncomfortable, not because they're wrong, but because they're right in ways you can't debate away in a meeting.

THE FOUR THAT MATTER

There's a short list of metrics that correlate with delivery performance. You'll recognise them if your team has ever read the DORA or SPACE research. But theory aside, the value is practical, operational, and immediate.

• **Lead Time for Changes**

Measured from the first commit to the production deploy. Shorter lead times mean faster iteration, tighter feedback loops, and lower coordination costs. If it takes ten days to ship a two-line fix, your system is lying to you.

• **Deployment Frequency**

How often does working code reach production? Weekly? Daily? Hourly? The cadence reflects the system's health and the team's confidence. Frequency is less about speed than it is about flow.

- **Change Failure Rate**

How often do those deployments cause breakage? Not in theory, but in real terms: rollbacks, incidents, pagers, user reports. A high rate here signals fragility; a low rate, coupled with a high deployment frequency, signals maturity.

- **Mean Time to Recovery (MTTR)**

Once something fails, how fast do you recover? Recovery time doesn't just measure incident response. It measures how well you've instrumented your system, practised your rollbacks, and trained your team to act.

Together, these four form a tight feedback loop. They measure throughput, safety, speed, and resilience. They're hard to game. And they reveal something more profound: how much your team trusts its own delivery process.

THE METRICS THAT DON'T

And then there's the other list. The ones that linger on dashboards like expired milk in the fridge: tolerated, never questioned, never consumed.

- **Velocity**

Beloved by managers. Feared by teams. Irrelevant to customers. Velocity isn't a delivery metric. It's a budgeting tool for time that's already gone.

- **Story Points Completed**

A fiction built atop another fiction. If story points are arbitrary, then point totals are fantasy accounting.

- **Bug Counts**

Bug counts reflect process, not product. Teams that track bugs obsessively often miss the real issue: why are users reporting them first?

- **Lines of Code**

Still tracked. Still meaningless. The fastest way to double this number is to write worse code.

- **Number of Commits**

Commits are effort, not outcome. And they inflate easily with formatting changes and overzealous linters.

These metrics don't illuminate. They anaesthetise. They give middle management something to present, but they don't help teams improve.

And here's the kicker: **any metric that requires engineers to change their behaviour to improve the number is already flawed**.

THE PURPOSE OF METRICS IS NAVIGATION, NOT JUDGMENT

Good metrics serve the team. They clarify direction. They highlight improvement. They trigger an investigation when something shifts unexpectedly.

Bad metrics, on the other hand, become tools of control. They drive performance theatre. They reward manipulation. They erode trust.

The distinction is simple:

- A healthy team looks at MTTR and says, *How do we make that faster?*
- A dysfunctional one looks at velocity and says, *Can you double it this sprint?*

Metrics aren't levers to pull. They're dials to observe. They don't fix anything. They tell you what's changing and where to look next.

If your metrics create fear, they're not metrics, they're surveillance.

QUIET METRICS, REAL IMPROVEMENT

The most powerful metrics are often the most boring. They don't sparkle. They don't trend on Slack. However, they exhibit slow, consistent progress over time or early warning signs that something is fraying.

When a team embraces meaningful measurement:

- They catch delivery bottlenecks early.
- They spot the test suite decay before it becomes friction.
- They notice rising rollback frequency and investigate root causes.
- They reduce incident resolution time not with pep talks, but with practice.

None of this feels impressive in the moment. But over quarters and years, it defines a high-performance culture.

INSTRUMENT EVERYTHING. REPORT SELECTIVELY.

Modern tools make it trivially easy to measure everything. PR size, cycle time, code ownership dispersion, test flake rates, deploy durations — the data is there. And you should capture it.

But capturing data is not the same as acting on it.

The golden rule is simple:

Track broadly. Act narrowly.

You won't know what matters until something breaks. But when it does, that trace data becomes invaluable.

What you want is a rich observability trail on your own process. Not to broadcast. To learn.

The best dashboards are rarely shared during all-hands meetings. They're quiet tools, reviewed by the people doing the work, not performing it.

FINAL THOUGHT: MEASURE WHAT YOU'D MISS IF IT BROKE

This is the litmus test.

If a metric turned red tomorrow, and your team wouldn't notice it (in incidents, in feedback loops, or in recovery speed) then it wasn't worth tracking in the first place.

The best teams don't just measure for the sake of measurement. They measure because they **ship constantly**, and they want to know why things slow down, why things break, and how they can improve.

They don't ask for perfect metrics, just honest ones.

And that's enough.

CHAPTER 12
DELIVERY IS NOT THE DESTINATION

Somewhere between the third successful deploy of the morning and your sixth celebratory Slack emoji, you need to ask a tricky question:

Did any of this matter?

It's seductive to equate shipping with progress. The pipeline is green. The tests passed. The deploy logs are clean. Something changed in production.

But unless that change *landed* — unless it was seen, used, or felt by a human being with a problem — it might as well have been a commit to /dev/null.

This chapter is not about slowing down. It's about finishing the job.

OUTPUT VS. OUTCOME

High-functioning teams obsess over deploys. Great teams obsess over outcomes.

Delivery is an engineering milestone. But value delivery is a system outcome. If your systems are humming but adoption is flat, you're not moving forward. You're just moving.

Shipping should not be confused with success. There are plenty of fast-moving teams shipping code that never touches reality. Software isn't a manufacturing process, it's a feedback system. Every release is a hypothesis. Every user interaction is a data point. Until you treat it that way, you're just increasing entropy.

Ask yourself:

- Did the new feature improve a core metric?
- Did it reduce a user's pain point?

- Did it teach us anything we didn't already know?

If the answer is "we don't know," you're operating a well-oiled factory with no idea what the customers ordered.

THE FEEDBACK SURFACE

You own your deploys. Good. Now own your impact.

Modern observability stacks can tell you more than just whether a service is up and running. They can tell you:

- Who's using the feature.
- How often they engage.
- Where they drop off.
- What breaks, silently.

But raw data isn't insight. Developers must learn to read the signals that matter. A sudden drop in engagement is as urgent as a memory leak. A feature no one uses is a bug in disguise.

These are not vanity metrics. They're signals. Your software is trying to speak. Stop muting it.

INSTRUMENT FOR LEARNING, NOT JUST FAILURE

You already log errors. Good. Now log the absence. Log neglect. Log abandonment.

Failures aren't always exceptions. Sometimes, the silence is the loudest signal.

Example:

- You built a new onboarding flow. See how many users complete it.
- You released a dashboard refresh. Log how many users bounce in under five seconds.
- You added a filter tool. Track if it's ever used twice.

When a deploy goes out, you should be listening not only for crashes but for indifference. Code that compiles is table stakes. Code that connects is the objective measure.

The signal isn't in uptime. It's in uptake.

THE FEATURE THAT DIDN'T MATTER

Every codebase has them. Deployed with pride. Never used. Eventually commented out with shame.

These aren't just wasted effort. They're noise in the system. Every unused feature adds:

- Cognitive load.
- UI friction.
- Maintenance cost.

Features that gather dust slow everyone else down. They clutter your APIs, pollute your telemetry, and confuse your users.

Shipping doesn't validate a feature. Usage does.

If no one touches it, rip it out. If it didn't change anything, learn faster next time. Velocity without learning is just inertia with CI.

TACTICALLY SPEAKING

Here's how to close the feedback loop:

- Tag every deploy with a question: What will we learn from this?"
- Include product metrics in post-deploy reviews. Not just latency or error rate. Feature use. Flow completion. Behaviour change.
- Monitor user behaviour as part of release health. Success isn't just "no alerts." It's "measurable impact."
- Make value a part of your definition of 'done'. Done = Deployed + Adopted + Understood.

FINAL THOUGHT: THE COMMIT ISN'T THE VICTORY

The green checkmark isn't the win. The real win is quieter:

- The user who finds something finally easy.
- The support ticket that never had to be written.
- The feature that becomes invisible because it just works.

Until you measure that, you haven't shipped. You've just typed faster than most.

So yes, deploy often. But measure what lands. Because delivery isn't the destination. It's the beginning of your feedback loop.

CHAPTER 13
PRODUCT AWARENESS AS AN ENGINEERING DISCIPLINE

The software world is saturated with cross-functional theatre. Alignment decks. Endless backlog grooming. Product syncs that feel like hostage videos.

But there is a core truth buried under the nonsense:

Engineering is not separate from the product. It is a product, made executable.

Every function in a modern SaaS team is upstream or downstream of user value. Code is only valuable when it becomes a user experience. This is not a dilution of engineering purity. It is its highest calling.

You don't need to be a product manager. However, you do need to care if the things you build are real, useful, and of good quality.

QUIET AWARENESS BEATS LOUD ALIGNMENT

Real product awareness isn't about meetings. It's about signal detection.

Engineers sit closer to the fire than anyone. They see:

- The error logs from edge cases that no one imagined.
- The unused API calls.
- The support chat integrations no one updates.
- The usage metrics that dip after design changes.

This is product research, whether or not anyone labels it as such. Ignore it, and you're flying blind. Tune into it, and you build with intuition that no roadmap can replicate.

Awareness means being mindful of consequences, not just following instructions. It means noticing when a minor feature causes unexpected delight, or when a redesign quietly disrupts a power user's workflow.

The best engineers are not the loudest in product syncs. They're the ones who notice, synthesise, and adjust. They make better decisions not because they were told, but because they *knew where to look.*

BUILD OBSERVABILITY FOR BEHAVIOUR, NOT JUST BREAKAGE

Most teams stop at instrumentation for crashes, latency, or 500s. Few go further.

What if your dashboards also showed:

- Which button is never clicked?
- Which feature gets turned off immediately after use?
- Which flow is abandoned halfway 80% of the time?

This isn't creepy. It's craftsmanship.

You're not mining users. You're watching your code in the wild and asking, *'Did this help?' Did this land? Did we get it right?*

Sound engineering asks: Did it compile? Did it deploy? Excellent engineering adds: did it matter? Did it work for the user?

Behavioural observability is not a product luxury. It is an engineering necessity in any modern stack where the gap between commit and customer is measured in hours.

FEATURE TOGGLES ARE PRODUCT TOOLS

Feature flags aren't just safety valves. They're microscopes.

Gradual rollouts let you see what resonates before committing. A/B toggles let you learn what works before refactoring. Kill switches let you admit a mistake before it compounds.

Used well, they let you deploy with confidence *and* curiosity.

- Turn it on for 5% and measure engagement.
- Try variant A in the EU, variant B in the US.
- Roll back quietly if the bounce rate spikes.

Toggles give you the precision to test without fear. They are the proving ground between hypothesis and habit.

Engineers with this mindset aren't just shipping. They're *testing hypotheses in code*. They treat every flag as a temporary probe: "Does this solve what we thought it would?"

It is not enough to know if a system can run. We must know if the system is *right*.

PAIR WITH PRODUCT WITHOUT PRETENDING TO BE ONE

You don't need to write OKRs or host discovery calls. But you do need to:

- Ask what problem the ticket is intended to solve.
- Challenge assumptions when metrics aren't defined.
- Surface user friction you spot in the logs.
- Flag features that aren't performing as expected.

The most productive engineering-product relationships are not transactional. They're not waterfall. They're conversational. Each side brings signals. The shared goal is not "alignment", it's *clarity of purpose*.

The best PMs aren't gatekeepers. They're signal routers. Meet them there.

Treat product feedback like a test failure: curious, impersonal, and urgent. When a user drops out of a flow you've just shipped, investigate it as if it were a production bug.

ENGINEERING MATURITY INCLUDES PRODUCT EMPATHY

At some point, your technical excellence must evolve from:

- *"Did we ship cleanly?"* to
- *"Did it make anything better?"

The shift is quiet but powerful.

Senior engineers know that elegant code no one uses is indistinguishable from broken code.

Engineering maturity means you don't just fix bugs. You retire features that shouldn't exist. You shrink the surface area of complexity. You build less, better, with purpose.

A team that practices product empathy:

- Builds instrumentation by default.
- Tags deploys with hypotheses.
- Revisits decisions when user signals are weak.
- Refuses to build when the value is unclear.

You don't need to be a PM. But you do need to listen.

FINAL THOUGHT: RESPECT THE SIGNAL

Your systems talk. Your users talk. Even your unused features talk.

A mature engineer doesn't wait for Jira to tell them what matters. They *watch for what already is.*

Because the product is not a stakeholder, it serves as the medium. And every line you write becomes part of its voice.

Craft accordingly.

CHAPTER 14
PSYCHOLOGICAL SAFETY AND ACCOUNTABILITY
THE UNEXPECTED COEXISTENCE

Somewhere along the way, teams started treating "blameless" as a synonym for "consequence-free."

It wasn't meant to be.

Blamelessness was supposed to reduce fear, not responsibility.

But like many well-intentioned ideas, it got diluted. First into process language, then into culture theatre. Now it shows up in incident reviews as a kind of ritualised denial:

"No one's at fault. Nothing could have been done differently. Let's move on."

Except… things did go wrong.

And yes, something could have been done differently.

Let's be clear: psychological safety is essential. But so is accountability.

One without the other is either toxic or useless. Together, they build resilient teams.

WHAT PSYCHOLOGICAL SAFETY ACTUALLY MEANS

It doesn't mean you never feel uncomfortable. It doesn't mean all feedback is positive. It doesn't mean every idea gets equal weight.

Psychological safety means this:

- You can raise concerns without fear of punishment.
- You can admit mistakes without social fallout.
- You can challenge decisions, even loudly held ones, without career risk.

It's the condition that allows technical truth to surface.

And it's the reason high-performing teams have fewer silent disasters.

However, psychological safety is not a license to disengage. It's not an excuse to avoid tension. It's not a guarantee that your code won't be questioned, your logic won't be debated, or your incident won't require hard introspection.

The presence of safety doesn't remove discomfort. It makes discomfort productive.

THE ROLE OF ACCOUNTABILITY

Accountability often gets framed as blame with better branding. That's lazy thinking.

Real accountability isn't punitive. It's grounded. It means that actions have consequences, not punishments, but follow-through.

- If your service went down, you're part of the postmortem.
- If you shipped the bug, you own the rollback and the fix.
- If your alert caused a false positive, you will revise it.

This doesn't mean shame. It means participation. You don't get benched. You get involved.

The goal isn't to assign fault. The goal is to ensure that what happened doesn't happen again and that the people closest to the problem are empowered to prevent it from happening again.

WHERE IT GOES WRONG

When teams conflate safety with comfort, they stop asking hard questions. When they confuse accountability with blame, they begin to hide information.

The result is the same: systems degrade silently.

Incidents repeat.

Feedback dies in the hallway.

You get a team that's friendly, even supportive, but not effective.

You also get fragile confidence. Because the moment something serious happens, no one knows how to speak plainly.

WHAT A HEALTHY CULTURE LOOKS LIKE

The strongest teams aren't fearless. They're fear-literate. They don't avoid tension, they know how to use it constructively.

You'll notice:

- Incidents are reviewed openly, with specific contributions named and owned.
- Junior engineers feel safe raising concerns about senior decisions.
- Feedback is common, direct, and delivered without theatrics.
- Successes are celebrated, but not exaggerated.
- Mistakes are dissected, not moralised.

The question isn't: *Who messed up?*

The question is: *How did this happen?*

And then: *What will we change?*

WRITE THE POSTMORTEM FOR THE NEXT TEAM

The best postmortems are written not for compliance, but for continuity.

They're written so that the next engineer — months from now, mid-deploy, in a fog of partial context — understands what failed and why.

This means naming what broke. And who made what decision. Not to assign guilt. But to create a usable trail of context.

- What signals were missed?
- What assumptions proved false?
- What mitigations weren't in place?
- What trade-offs were accepted — and by whom?

This is what accountability looks like. Not punishment. Documentation.

It's not "blameless." It's *useful.*

FINAL THOUGHT: SAFETY WITHOUT ACCOUNTABILITY IS SENTIMENT. ACCOUNTABILITY WITHOUT SAFETY IS FEAR.

You need both.

Safety gives people the courage to speak.

Accountability gives that speech direction.

The goal isn't a culture free of conflict.

It's a culture where conflict refines, not corrodes.

And in that tension — well-managed, well-held — is where the best software is written.

Not just functional code. But durable, human systems.

The kind that stay calm.

And get better.

Even after things break.

CHAPTER 15
ORGANISATIONAL STRUCTURE AS TECH DEBT

Most teams treat architecture as something they can design and implement.

They treat organisational structure as something they inherited.

This is backwards.

Your org chart is the most powerful (and most ignored) architecture diagram in the company. It shapes how decisions are made, how systems are built, and how work flows (or doesn't). And like bad code, if left unchecked, it starts to rot.

The result? Slow teams. Noisy dependencies. Half-ownership of everything and whole-ownership of nothing.

Let's not be subtle here: **if your team structure doesn't match your system architecture, your system will suffer or your people will (usually both).**

CONWAY'S LAW ISN'T OPTIONAL

In 1968, Mel Conway wrote a paper that's still being ignored:

"Organisations design systems which mirror their own communication structures."

It was later dubbed *Conway's Law*, which is unfortunate, because calling it a "law" makes people think it's theoretical. It isn't.

It's gravity.

If your organisation is divided into front-end and back-end teams, your product will likely reflect that division, often with latency and blame between them.

If your teams are aligned by function, your systems will be functionally isolated, even when they shouldn't be.

And if you have a matrix structure, with one manager for delivery and another for "career growth", then congratulations. You've invented indecision.

Systems grow to match the conversations around them. And every unnecessary meeting is a signal that your structure isn't honest.

THE COST OF POOR ALIGNMENT

When your team structure doesn't reflect your architecture:

- Incidents require five people from three teams to triage.
- No one owns the whole user experience, just fragments.
- Dependencies slow delivery more than tech ever could.
- Teams begin to optimise for local clarity, not global outcome.

Worse, work becomes bureaucratic by design. Simple questions („Who owns this endpoint?") require detective work. Engineers build defensively, not creatively. Systems degrade in silence because no one feels truly responsible.

This isn't just about morale. It's about throughput.

Structure creates friction. And the wrong structure makes that friction feel inevitable.

WHEN TO RESTRUCTURE

You don't need a reorg every quarter. But you do need a pulse check.

Ask:

- Are our services structured the way our teams are?
- Can one team own a feature from concept to deployment?
- Do teams talk more internally than across boundaries?
- Does our escalation path match the failure path?

If the answers are no or unclear, then your structure is drifting.

You'll start to notice unusual behaviours. Teams optimising for metrics that don't help users. Dependencies formalised in handover tickets. "Shared ownership" that means shared avoidance.

None of this is malicious. It's emergent, which is why it has to be managed, not ignored.

AUTONOMY IS NOT ANARCHY

The solution isn't flattening the org chart or pretending everyone's a startup within a startup. Autonomy without coordination is just fragmentation.

But healthy structures do something specific: **they create complete responsibility within clearly bounded domains.**

This means:

- Each team owns a complete slice of functionality: front to back, dev to deploy.
- Internal APIs are versioned, documented, and stable.
- Teams can ship independently, but stay aligned through contracts, not consensus.

This doesn't mean fewer standards. It means fewer surprises.

Autonomy isn't freedom from process. It's freedom from interference.

AVOIDING MATRIX MADNESS

The matrix model was invented for good reasons: to promote resource efficiency, facilitate flexible staffing, and leverage shared expertise. But it tends to collapse under its ambiguity.

When people report to multiple managers, or have to serve numerous initiatives, they quickly lose track of which goal is real.

Matrix structures breed the following:

- Conflicting priorities disguised as "alignment meetings"
- Delayed feedback loops across reporting lines
- Multiple layers of vague accountability
- Performance reviews that depend on proxy opinions

If your engineers need to navigate a PowerPoint to understand who they work with, you don't have structure — you have inertia.

FINAL THOUGHT: STRUCTURE IS A FORM OF CODE

You don't version-control your org chart. But you should treat it with the same discipline.

- Clear ownership
- Explicit boundaries
- Refactor when brittle
- Simplify when possible

Every misaligned team boundary introduces cognitive load.

Every extra hop in communication introduces latency.

Every orphaned service introduces risk.

Your team topology is not a decision made in the background. It's one of the few strategic levers you control.

Pull it deliberately.

Refactor it often.

And above all, make it match the system you're trying to build.

CHAPTER 16
QUIET SYSTEMS AT SCALE

Speed makes noise. Scale makes silence fragile.

It's easy to build fast when you're small. It's easy to ship often when you're scrappy. However, when the company grows — with more people, more layers, and more systems — things start to fray. Not because anyone got lazy, but because complexity compounds quietly.

Most orgs deal with this by adding a process. And then the process for the process. Soon, you've got councils, boards, handoffs, and checklists. What was once fast is now "managed." What was once elegant is now tolerated.

But scale doesn't have to mean ceremony.

The best teams don't grow noisier as they scale.

They grow quieter because they've built the habits that *survive scale.*

WHY "MOVE FAST" BECOMES "MOVE WELL"

In the early days, speed is your weapon. You can out-ship your competitors. You can turn on a dime. You can deploy ten times a day with barely a conversation.

However, at scale, raw speed can break things. A slight misalignment in a startup is a Slack thread. The exact misalignment in a scaled org becomes a customer outage, a support surge, a postmortem with ten people and zero conclusions.

So the language changes.

From fast → to *reliable.*

From responsive → to *resilient.*

From heroic → to *systemic*.

This isn't slowness. It's maturity.

Speed still matters, but it's no longer about how fast you type. It's about how well your system absorbs change.

WHAT QUIET LOOKS LIKE

Quiet doesn't mean idle. It means composed. It means that change flows through the system without friction, without escalation, without drama.

You'll know you've reached it when:

- Deployments happen daily, and no one makes a big deal.
- Incident reviews are short, factual, and improve something real.
- Feature rollouts happen in stages, behind toggles, without announcement.
- Developers aren't waiting on each other. Or waiting at all.
- Meetings are short. Dashboards are trusted. Slack isn't on fire.

This is not "high alignment." It's **low friction**.

Not a culture of consensus, but one of clarity.

Quiet systems don't mean fewer changes.

They mean less chaos per change.

HOW TO PRESERVE DISCIPLINE AS YOU SCALE

The most considerable risk in a scaling organisation isn't bad code. It's organisational drift.

You start with one engineering team. They follow the playbook. They deploy from trunk, test their own code, and build observability into everything. It works.

Then the second team spins up. And the third. Then someone builds a new service using "what worked at their last company." Then you hire a QA engineer, and suddenly the testing culture regresses. Then you onboard a new platform tool that doesn't match your conventions.

It's not sabotage. It's entropy.

And unless you act, it becomes the new normal.

What works at scale is **discipline with flexibility**:

- Shared principles, local autonomy
- Clear defaults, overridable with reason

- Guardrails over gates

You can't template everything. But you can hold the line on what matters:

- Every service has an owner.
- Every commit goes through the pipeline.
- Every deploy is observable.
- Every incident results in a change.

This isn't about central control. It's about central clarity.

THE COMPANY THAT GREW WITHOUT SHOUTING

At one fintech startup, the first two engineers built everything on trunk-based development, with full test ownership and a deploy-on-merge culture. By the time they reached fifty engineers, nothing had changed, because every new hire was onboarded into that rhythm.

Their delivery velocity didn't increase with size. It stayed flat. But it stayed *flat at high throughput*. More teams, same number of deploys per engineer, same MTTR, same rollback safety.

The magic wasn't in the tools. It was in what *didn't* change.

The process was strong enough not to require reinvention.

And quiet enough not to be resented.

They didn't call it a framework.

They just called it "how we build things."

THE PARADOX OF CALM VELOCITY

You'll notice something strange in high-performing orgs:

They don't talk about performance.

They talk about user behaviour. System behaviour. Incident patterns. But not "how agile" they are. They don't fill retros with discussion of ticket flow. They don't brag about cycle times.

Because they don't need to.

They move fast, without calling it that.

They release often, without ceremonies.

They recover quickly, without drama.

This is calm velocity: the state where systems are built for change, teams are practised in change, and no one panics when change comes.

It feels underwhelming. That's how you know it's working.

FINAL THOUGHT: SCALE SHOULD WIDEN CONFIDENCE, NOT DILUTE IT

Too many teams grow headcount and lose nerve.

They add layers instead of clarity. They drown in their own processes.

But the best ones? They stay sharp. They stay lean, not in structure, but in posture.

Because the real win isn't building a fast team.

It's building a team that stays fast as it grows.

And when that happens, the system gets quieter, not because less is happening, but because it's finally happening *well*.

CHAPTER 17
AI IN THE SDLC
A TOOL, NOT A CRUTCH

There's a moment, in every new wave of tooling, when excitement overtakes clarity.

This is that moment for AI.

The hype is understandable. Never before have we seen tools that can write code, generate tests, summarise documentation, and suggest architecture, all in seconds. The demos are dazzling. The potential is enormous. The temptation is simple: let it work.

But there's a difference between help and handover.

There's a difference between tools that serve thinking and tools that replace it.

And in that gap lies the future of software engineering.

Used wisely, AI enhances clarity.

Used passively, it erodes competence.

Because what AI offers isn't mastery. It's completion.

And those aren't the same thing.

WHERE AI EXCELS

Let's not diminish its strengths. AI does many things well — in some cases, astoundingly well. But these things share a theme: they're bounded, patterned, and free from ambiguity.

AI thrives in the spaces where the rules are clear, the input is clean, and the outcome is primarily mechanical.

- **Code Completion**

Autocomplete, once a trivial productivity feature, is now a collaborator. It fills in loops, closes branches, and writes test scaffolding. This is not intelligence. It's a statistically informed prediction and it saves time.

- **Test Suggestions**

Given a function, AI can propose edge cases, generate stubs, and expose basic assumptions. For legacy systems with minimal coverage, this alone can improve quality. Think of it as hygiene: not perfect, but protective.

- **Log Analysis and Anomaly Detection**

Where humans drown in logs, AI can cluster, summarise, and point to the unusual. It's not a diagnosis, but triage. The system flags "this looks wrong," and that's enough to accelerate the human response.

- **Translation and Documentation**

From one language to another. From cryptic APIs to coherent summaries. From engineer notes to onboarding materials. AI can help make internal systems legible.

- **Bulk Refactoring at Scale**

You want to rename a pattern across dozens of services? Modern LLM tools can assist. Cautiously. Repetitively. Usefully.

All of this frees mental bandwidth. Not to think less, but to think more about the things that matter.

But only if we use the time well.

WHERE AI FAILS — AND ALWAYS WILL

The failure points of AI aren't bugs. They're design limitations. AI does not understand. It correlates. It does not reason. It imitates.

That distinction matters.

- **Judgment**

Engineering is a series of trade-offs. Should we optimise for performance or readability? Is now the right time to simplify this module, or do we wait until the quarter ends? Should we tolerate this workaround or revisit the design?

AI has no opinion. Because it has no stake.

- **Context Awareness**

AI does not know your customer. It does not know your company's risk tolerance. It does not know which feature was rushed for a deadline and which one supports 80% of your revenue. It can't distinguish between a code smell and a deliberate compromise. Context lives in people, not prompts.

- **Technical Taste**

This is the hardest to explain and the easiest to feel. Taste is what makes one engineer's solution clean and another's convoluted. It's what separates elegant architecture from premature abstraction. It's not taught. It's absorbed through years of mistakes and revisions.

AI hasn't earned any of that.

- **Ambiguity Handling**

When requirements are unclear (and they usually are) AI guesses. Sometimes correctly. Sometimes not. But it doesn't say, "This doesn't make sense." It doesn't push back. It doesn't ask questions. It just outputs something that looks plausible.

- **Ethical Decisions**

Should we collect this telemetry? Is it fair to automate this part of the system? Will this suggestion introduce bias or lock-in? These aren't coding questions. They're value questions. And AI doesn't have values.

The danger isn't that AI will take over. It's that we'll start to assume it knows best, not because it's right, but because it's fast and confident.

Which, come to think of it, describes many bad engineers as well.

THE HUMAN ROLE, REDEFINED — NOT REMOVED

The presence of AI shifts what it means to be a software engineer. But it doesn't reduce the need for one.

In fact, as AI improves, humans become increasingly important.

Because the tasks AI can't do — probably won't ever do — are the ones that define real engineering:

- Seeing the whole shape of a problem, across people, systems, and incentives.
- Navigating legacy decisions with empathy and pragmatism.
- Choosing simplicity over cleverness, even when cleverness is easier to generate.
- Teaching junior engineers *why* something matters, not just *how* it's done.
- Designing systems with the future in mind, not just the ticket in front of you.

These are human skills. And they don't get automated.

They get sharpened. Or forgotten.

The engineer of 2025 doesn't need to type faster. They need to **discern** faster.

What to keep. What to ignore. What to rewrite. What to leave alone.

AI AS MULTIPLIER, NOT SUBSTITUTE

Treat AI as a junior partner — fast, tireless, and eager to help. But do not hand it the wheel. It's a multiplier. If your team is already thoughtful, it amplifies quality. If your team is chaotic, it just ships chaos faster.

In other words:

- AI + good process = acceleration
- AI + bad process = disaster
- AI + no process = entropy in disguise

The mistake isn't using AI. The mistake is assuming it's neutral. It reflects your habits, your assumptions, your blind spots — at scale.

So ask yourself:

- Who reviews the AI's output?
- What standards guide its suggestions?
- Are we using it to explore or to defer thinking?
- Do we understand the cost of a wrong suggestion?

Because AI can suggest hundreds of solutions.

But only humans live with the consequences.

FINAL THOUGHT: DON'T BUILD A TEAM THAT FORGETS HOW TO THINK

This is the real risk.

Not job loss. Not singularity fantasies. Not "AI is coming for the engineers."

The risk is internal: that teams become overly dependent on AI support, losing their own fluency. That they stop teaching fundamentals. That junior engineers never learn to debug without a prompt. That systems become full of plausible but unexamined code.

In short, that thinking becomes a premium skill.

When it used to be table stakes.

So use AI. Absolutely. Let it help. Let it accelerate. Let it catch what you missed. But do not let it think for you. Because the one thing AI cannot replicate, the thing that defines your craft, is care.

And care, like quality, can't be pasted in.

CHAPTER 18
ONBOARDING FOR MODERN ENGINEERING

Most onboarding programs are theatre. You receive a Notion document, a shared calendar, and a week filled with polite meetings. By the end, your new engineer knows which Slack channel to mute, which manager to avoid, and which build step occasionally fails without reason. But they still don't know how to ship.

The problem isn't documentation. It's a drift. The further a team deviates from its founding practices, the more it begins to treat delivery principles like folklore. Onboarding becomes passive. Engineers "figure it out" by observing others' struggles.

Modern engineering demands more. Not more content. More precision.

In high-performing teams, onboarding isn't just a ritual. It's a test.

STOP FRAMING IT AS "RAMP-UP TIME"

Most organisations give new hires a grace period: a few weeks of slow progress, shadowing, and perhaps fixing a typo or two. It feels humane. But it teaches the wrong lesson. That production is sacred. That errors are to be feared. That autonomy is a reward, not a requirement.

Modern teams do the opposite:

- **New engineers deploy in their first week.** Even a doc fix, even behind a toggle. Doesn't matter. The pipeline must become familiar.
- **Mentors review, not protect.** You're not shielding them. You're showing them the guardrails and then handing them the wheel.
- **The goal isn't comfort. It's fluency.** The faster someone moves through the real delivery process, the sooner they become a contributor instead of a liability.

This isn't harsh. It's honest. And in systems built for safety, there's no reason to delay trust.

MODEL THE BEHAVIOUR YOU WANT REPEATED

Telling someone to "test their code" is less effective than reviewing their PR and asking why there's no log line for the failure path.

Good onboarding is imitation:

- **Show how you commit.** Clear messages, tight scope, no nonsense.
- **Show how you test.** Not just what tests you wrote, but why.
- **Show how you observe.** Deploy something, then open the dashboard. Teach telemetry as storytelling.

Every action is a signal. If you batch up work in a feature branch for three days, they will too. If you rerun flaky tests without fixing them, so will they. Culture isn't taught. It's watched.

DON'T TEACH SAFETY. BUILD IT IN.

New engineers shouldn't fear deploys. They shouldn't fear breaking things. If they do, the system is the problem, not them.

Modern systems are:

- **Toggle-rich**: nothing gets exposed unless someone decides it should.
- **Well-tested**: regressions are identified before they reach production.
- **Observable**: alerts and logs tell the truth, early and loudly.

If the pipeline is brittle, onboarding becomes superstition. If the deployment is painful, learning becomes a fear.

So make it safe. Not through handbooks. Through defaults.

CREATE A RHYTHM, NOT A CURRICULUM

Most onboarding decks are forgotten within a week. But a rhythm? That lasts.

- **Weekly delivery goals.** Not huge, not arbitrary. Just enough to keep motion visible.
- **Slack rituals.** End-of-day updates, no status theatre. Share what was learned, blocked, and unblocked.
- **Pairing, not presentations.** Watch them code. Let them watch you debug. That's real onboarding.

You're not teaching doctrine. You're installing tempo.

FINAL THOUGHT: FIRST IMPRESSIONS AREN'T CULTURAL. THEY'RE PROCEDURAL.

When someone joins your team, they don't absorb your values. They absorb your defaults.

So if your team:

- Commits often
- Tests deliberately
- Deploys calmly
- Investigates observability with curiosity

...then that's what the new engineer becomes.

Onboarding isn't orientation. It's transmission. And like every system worth building, it should be fast, fault-tolerant, and quietly effective.

CHAPTER 19
PRODUCT, UX, AND QUIET COLLABORATION

Engineering isn't a factory. The product isn't a request queue. And UX isn't a paint job.

But in too many teams, that's exactly how things play out. Engineers build in isolation. Designers push Figma into the void. Product managers shuttle tickets like air traffic controllers with no radar. Everyone is "aligned" on paper and confused in practice.

Modern delivery demands something else: a low-friction rhythm between disciplines. Not a consensus. Not a ceremony. Just quiet, informed collaboration.

STOP SHIPPING PRESENTATIONS

In traditional orgs, product specs read like pitches. Slides, mockups, "target outcomes." They get reviewed, signed off, and delivered like blueprints. Then, engineering builds something almost like it. Then UX patches the gaps. Then users do something nobody predicted.

Modern teams skip the theatre:

- **Design prototypes in the same sprint in which they're implemented.** Nothing lives in pre-dev purgatory.
- **Experiment early.** Behind toggles, to cohorts, with real users. Feedback beats opinion.
- **Refine post-ship.** MVP doesn't mean lowest effort. It means the fastest route to clarity.

If your spec can't survive contact with a real user, it wasn't a spec. It was a sketch.

TREAT UX FRICTION AS TELEMETRY

Most observability focuses on the backend: response time, error rate, and saturation.

But user friction is just as tangible, just as measurable, and often more valuable.

- **Instrument UI behaviour.** Clicks, time on screen, abort patterns.
- **Tag features by intent.** What journey is this part of? What question does it answer?
- **Log hesitation.** If users hover, backtrack, or stall, that's a signal.

Every confused user is a metric you didn't track. Start listening.

CO-DEFINE "DONE"

Ask an engineer, a product manager, and a designer what "done" means. You'll get three answers and a meeting invite.

Modern teams collapse that ambiguity:

- **Done means observable.** If it doesn't log or emit metrics, it's not done.
- **Done means reversible.** Can we toggle it off without regret?
- **Done means usable.** Not just functional, but fit-for-purpose.

You don't need a definition of done. You need a shared checklist, tied to delivery behaviour.

WORK IN THE SAME RHYTHM

This is where most collaboration fails: mismatched tempos.

- Product plans monthly.
- UX iterates weekly.
- Engineering ships daily.

That desynchronisation leads to bottlenecks, resentment, and late surprises.

So align not on ceremony, but on cadence:

- **Weekly demos, not reviews.** Show what changed. Ask what matters next.
- **Shared backlog hygiene.** If it can't be built in a week, break it.
- **Cross-functional pairing.** A designer and an engineer on the same Zoom, fixing spacing in code. That's speed.

You're not building a process. You're syncing a pulse.

FINAL THOUGHT: STOP COLLABORATING. START CO-CREATING.

Most organisations try to improve collaboration by adding steps, such as more handoffs, more syncs, and more alignment.

But genuine collaboration isn't additive. It's subtractive.

Fewer artefacts. Fewer approvals. Fewer walls between those who imagine the product and those who build it.

The best products aren't designed, specced, and implemented. They're co-created, shipped behind toggles, and debugged in real time.

And no one argues about alignment because they're already moving in the same direction.

CHAPTER 20
MODERN ENGINEERING IN REGULATED ENVIRONMENTS

Most teams blame regulation for their inertia. "We can't ship fast, we're in healthcare." "Banking compliance won't allow continuous delivery." "Our auditors won't approve feature toggles."

The fundamental constraint isn't regulation. It's imagination.

Modern engineering works in regulated domains. It just requires discipline, auditability, and a refusal to conflate control with slowness. The challenge isn't that you're being watched. It's that your systems were never designed to be legible. And legibility—not speed—is what most regulators care about.

BUILD TRUST INTO THE PIPELINE

You don't need manual signoffs to be compliant. You need traceability that holds up under scrutiny.

- **Every commit tells a story.** Not just who, what, and when — but why. Make purpose part of the version history.
- **Tests are versioned alongside code.** There is no such thing as "test documentation" that lives separately.
- **Deployments are logged, signed, and reproducible.** Even in the most regulated environments, fast delivery is possible when you know exactly what went out, who approved it, and how to roll it back.
- **Rollback is not a plan B. It's a feature.** Compliance requires control. Reversibility is control.

Most compliance issues stem from data lineage problems. The auditor's nightmare isn't that something broke. It's that no one knows how, when, or why.

TREAT POLICY AS CODE

Audit trails, segregation of duties, approval workflows: humans often manage these with clipboards. And humans fail at scale.

- **Store control logic with the codebase.** If you need approvals for specific risk categories, model them explicitly.
- **Tag features by impact zones.** PII? Payment logic? Legal calculation? Tags make risk visible.
- **Use static analysis to enforce policy boundaries.** If a feature affects specific domains, escalate the issue before the merge.

A written process is not proof of enforcement. Code is.

Auditors don't care if you wrote a policy. They care whether your system makes it impossible to skip it.

DESIGN FOR AUDITABILITY FROM DAY ZERO

You can't retrofit audit trails. You can't paste a dashboard onto a chaotic legacy system and call it traceable.

Auditability needs to be a core design constraint:

- **Immutable logs.** Append-only, tamper-evident, time-synced. No shared Excel spreadsheets.
- **Event correlation.** If a payment was processed, what commit triggered it? What test covered it? What version of code handled it?
- **Standard naming and tagging.** If toggles, metrics, and logs follow consistent patterns, auditors stop digging.

When your logs are coherent, your engineers stop fearing audits. And your auditors stop fearing you.

USE TOGGLES. TRANSPARENTLY.

In regulated spaces, toggles are often viewed as a liability: a means to smuggle incomplete features past QA.

But that's not a toggle problem. That's a trust problem.

- **Toggle registries are mandatory.** Every toggle has an owner, a rationale, and a removal date.
- **Expose toggles to non-devs.** A dashboard that compliance and legal can browse.
- **Enforce toggle hygiene in CI.** Expired toggles block the pipeline.

Toggles are how you ship safely. And regulators love safety, when it's visible.

SEGREGATION OF DUTIES WITHOUT SEGREGATION OF TEAMS

The phrase "segregation of duties" is often misinterpreted as "developers must not touch prod."

In reality, it means controls must exist to prevent unilateral actions without oversight.

- **Use role-based permissions and multi-step approvals.** One person writes the code, another merges it.
- **Enforce peer review.** Not optional. Not social. A binding control.
- **Leverage audit-logging platforms.** Every action that affects production is logged and queryable.

You don't need a separate team to validate code. You need a system that makes misuse difficult and obvious.

MAP COMPLIANCE TO DELIVERY BEHAVIOUR

In most legacy orgs, audits are seasonal events. Compliance is something you "prepare for." Slides, spreadsheets, checklists.

This is inefficient. Worse: it breaks flow.

Modern teams treat audits as continuous validation:

- **Attach control metadata to tickets.** What regulation does this ticket intersect? Who validated the approach?
- **Autogenerate reports.** Build pipeline tooling that produces printable evidence for each release.
- **Involve compliance early.** Not just at release time, but at design time.

Every user story should be traceable from idea to production. If it's not, you're managing risk with hope.

DESIGN FOR INSPECTIONS, NOT AVOIDANCE

You can't avoid being inspected. But you can choose how painful that inspection is.

- **Make observability visible across functions.** Product, compliance, engineering — same dashboards.
- **Version everything.** Documentation, runbooks, checklists.
- **Train engineers in compliance language.** Not to appease bureaucracy, but to reason about risk.

A compliant team is not a slow team. It's a deliberate one. And a deliberate team can often ship faster than the reckless one, because it doesn't stop for panic reviews.

FINAL THOUGHT: REGULATION SLOWS THEATRE. NOT DELIVERY.

Most organisations use regulations as an excuse to maintain bad processes. Manual reviews. Spreadsheet traceability. Ticket ping-pong. Fear.

But regulation is rarely the actual bottleneck.

In fact, when practised well, it can become an accelerant. You start building legible systems. Reliable. Designed for inspection.

Modern engineering doesn't bypass regulation. It metabolises it.

Because if your systems are safe, reversible, observable, and traceable—you're already more compliant than most teams claiming to be.

CHAPTER 21
TRANSFORMING LEGACY SYSTEMS

Everyone wants a rewrite. Nobody wants the outage.

Legacy systems are the elephant in the sprint. Everyone tiptoes around them, blames them, and secretly dreams of replacing them. But replacing them outright is usually a fantasy and often a disaster. The more complex the system, the more embedded its quirks. What appears to be clutter is frequently business logic disguised as technical debt.

Modern engineering doesn't demand a clean slate. It requires quiet transformation: safe, observable, and strategically invisible. Instead of dramatic refactors and grand unveilings, you aim for a series of calm, deliberate shifts. No fanfare. Just momentum.

START WITH DECOUPLING, NOT REFACTORING

Your instinct might be to clean the code. Make it elegant, modular, and expressive. But this isn't about beauty. It's about containment.

- **Introduce APIs, not classes.** Create separation first, structure later.
- **Wrap dangerous zones with stable interfaces.** Think of it as digital sandbagging.
- **Surface dependencies explicitly.** If it's invisible, it's uncontrollable.

You can't clean what you haven't isolated.

TOGGLE AND SHADOW QUIETLY

Once you've decoupled, avoid the big switch. Introduce toggles. Run shadows. Verify in production, not theory.

- **Route a small percentage of traffic to the new path.** Measure it.
- **Compare outputs and performance silently.** Don't announce. Observe.
- **Log deviations.** Treat them as clues, not failures.

Users shouldn't notice. If they do, you've moved too fast.

MEASURE BEFORE YOU CHANGE

Legacy systems often contain features that no one uses and workflows that no one understands. Changing them unthinkingly is not bold, it's reckless.

- **Instrument usage.** Which parts are slow, fragile, or forgotten?
- **Kill softly.** Use toggles and logs before deletion.
- **Resist cosmetic cleanup.** Renaming haunted methods won't drive clarity.

Transform what matters. Leave the ghosts alone, for now.

AVOID THE REWRITE TAX

The cost of a rewrite is rarely technical. It's human.

- **Scope creep reintroduces old complexity.** The system did more than you thought.
- **Regression risk is real.** Old bugs return wearing new clothes.
- **Morale suffers.** Teams burn out rebuilding invisible value.

Safer path? Parallel execution.

- **Same interface, different internals.**
- **Old and new systems coexist.**
- **Celebrate deletions.** That's momentum.

You're not designing a replacement. You're staging a retreat.

KNOW WHEN TO CONTAIN

Not every legacy system needs fixing. Some need burial. Others just need space.

- **Wrap the low-risk, low-value systems.** Let them fade.
- **Stabilise brittle but critical paths.** Document, test, then refactor.
- **Only modernise what pays off.** Refactoring is not a virtue. It's a tactic.

FINAL THOUGHT: REWRITE WITH SCISSORS, NOT BULLDOZERS

Old code isn't evil. It's just unexplained. Often, the people who wrote it are no longer with us. The context is gone. The logs are silent.

Begin with understanding, not judgment. And when you move, move with precision:

- Name the dependencies.
- Wrap the danger zones.
- Toggle and shadow.
- Measure relentlessly.

The best legacy migrations aren't hero stories. They're quiet disappearances.

And when they're done, no one remembers the pain. Just the silence.

CHAPTER 22
THE SUBTLE SYSTEM

You can tell how a system was built by how it behaves under pressure. Some fracture. Others blame. Many panic, not because the situation is impossible, but because the structure was never truly designed; it was merely accumulated.

The best systems recover without commotion. No fireworks. No firefighting. Just a quiet shift back to equilibrium. No heroes needed.

This book has never been about individual genius. It has been about environments: the structures, constraints, and defaults that enable good software to happen and continue happening. Teams come and go. Trends evolve. But a well-constructed system outlasts both.

Sound systems aren't reactive. They're shaped deliberately, so that stability is the byproduct, not the aspiration.

THE SHAPE OF A QUIET SYSTEM

A quiet system doesn't mean a passive one. It means a composed one. One that absorbs complexity without amplifying it. Where friction is not avoided through heroics or culture decks, but is removed at the root by structural design.

You'll notice these systems not because someone tells you they're great, but because nothing feels fragile. Deployments aren't production. Incident responses aren't improvisation. Planning doesn't resemble a hostage negotiation.

Documentation exists and is used. Interfaces are stable. Change is expected, not exceptional. And while engineers still argue, because they care, the arguments are about decisions, not dysfunction.

In these environments:

- Pipelines don't require second-guessing.
- Incidents are reviewed without drama.
- Ownership is clear, not ceremonial.
- Deadlines reflect reality, not negotiation.

None of these emerge by accident. Each one reflects an intent: to make the right thing easier than the rushed thing. To make recovery simple. To remove ego from routine.

BEHAVIOUR, BY DESIGN

Engineers don't respond to slides. They react to constraints, defaults, and incentives. Systems that rely on motivation burn out their operators. Systems that depend on design and build consistency without heroism.

A well-engineered environment influences behaviour without declaring it. You don't need a poster to say "We value code quality" when the pull request template, review process, and testing culture already demand it.

Similarly, you don't need to tell people to write documentation if the system expects it as part of the work. Not a moral plea — just a normal step.

The point is not to enforce. The point is to encode.

When a system encodes the correct values, engineers don't have to be constantly reminded. They simply act within a frame that supports them.

RESILIENCE BY SIMPLICITY

Loud systems often mistake complexity for sophistication. They layer process upon process, review upon review, until no one remembers what problem they were initially trying to solve.

Quiet systems pursue clarity. They favour fewer moving parts and fewer assumptions. They reward resilience, not cleverness. They don't reduce complexity through abstraction, they avoid it through better defaults.

This doesn't mean avoiding tools or rejecting structure. It means choosing each layer consciously. If every meeting, every dashboard, and every alert has a clear function and exit condition, the system doesn't accumulate noise.

The result isn't silence in the literal sense. It's a signal without chaos, stability without stillness.

WHAT SURVIVES

All technology ages. Tools become obsolete. Teams get restructured. Leadership changes. But the bones of a good system — its clarity, its safety nets, its expectations — tend to outlive the components.

Over time, that shows up in the culture. Not the slogans, but the habits. You'll see it in how decisions are made, how trade-offs are discussed, and how junior engineers learn without relying on tribal knowledge. There's less ceremony and more signal. Less ambiguity, more responsibility.

Most importantly, it becomes easier to keep improving. The system doesn't resist change. It channels it.

That, more than any stack or methodology, is what makes an engineering environment sustainable.

FINAL THOUGHT: DESIGN FOR QUIET

No system stays quiet by default. Quiet is not absence, it is a result. It emerges when clarity outweighs chaos, when defaults do more than instructions, and when process is seen as scaffolding, not theatre.

There will always be pressure to go fast, to patch the visible, to focus on what's loudest. But lasting environments are built by those who ask the quieter questions: What's still unclear? What's too fragile? What keeps being explained instead of encoded?

Develop a system that facilitates answering these questions. Then improve it without fuss. And when you've done that, you won't need to say much.

Because a sound system speaks for itself, mostly by getting out of the way.

CHAPTER 23
RECOMMENDED READING

As it's likely this book pushed you to embark on a very exciting voyage (towards boring), you may need some more guidelines. Here's my curated list of recommendations.

PRINCIPLES OF MODERN DELIVERY

- ***Accelerate: The Science of Lean Software and DevOps*** – Nicole Forsgren, Jez Humble, Gene Kim: *The evidence-based foundation for high-performing software teams.*
- ***Team Topologies*** – Matthew Skelton & Manuel Pais*: A structural approach to building fast, flow-optimised organisations.*
- ***The Phoenix Project*** – Gene Kim, Kevin Behr, George Spafford*: A novelised, relatable introduction to DevOps and flow thinking.*

TECHNICAL PRACTICES WITH TEETH

- ***The Pragmatic Programmer*** – Andrew Hunt & David Thomas*: Enduring principles for software craft. Still hits hard.*
- ***Continuous Delivery*** – Jez Humble & David Farley: *The foundational text on CI/CD pipelines — long-winded but essential.*
- ***Building Microservices*** – Sam Newman: *A pragmatic guide to designing systems that scale sensibly.*
- ***Release It!*** – Michael T. Nygard: *Still the definitive book on building robust production systems.*

CULTURE, OWNERSHIP & TEAM DYNAMICS

- ***An Elegant Puzzle*** – Will Larson: *Thoughtful and tactical management of engineering orgs.*
- ***Radical Candor*** – Kim Scott: *For teams where psychological safety and honest feedback must coexist.*
- ***Debugging Teams*** – Brian W. Fitzpatrick & Ben Collins-Sussman: *An understated gem on the human side of engineering.*

OBSERVABILITY, TESTING & RELIABILITY

- ***Observability Engineering*** – Charity Majors, Liz Fong-Jones, George Miranda: *A practitioner's handbook for telemetry that matters.*
- ***Site Reliability Engineering*** – Google SRE team: *Dense, but canonical. Especially Chapter 3: "Embracing Risk."*
- ***Working Effectively with Legacy Code*** – Michael Feathers: *For when the subtle becomes the stubborn.*

FOR ENGINEERS WHO THINK IN SYSTEMS

- ***Thinking in Systems*** – Donella Meadows: *Not a software book — a mindset book. Required reading.*
- ***The Goal*** – Eliyahu M. Goldratt: *A manufacturing novel, but secretly the best book on flow in software.*
- ***Turn the Ship Around!*** – L. David Marquet: *Leadership by giving control, not taking it. Surprisingly applicable to dev teams.*

ABOUT THE AUTHOR

Lukasz Olczyk is a systems thinker, writer, and seasoned professional in the craft of software delivery. With over two decades of experience guiding complex projects across industries and borders, he brings a quiet clarity to chaotic environments and a steady hand to fast-moving teams.

Born in Poland and now settled in Germany, he prefers the patient arc of mastery over the noise of novelty. His approach blends technical depth with philosophical reflection, shaped as much by years in boardrooms as by solitary early mornings and long walks with a weighted rucksack.

He avoids spectacle, declines social media, and believes that excellence is better lived than displayed. His work, whether in code, conversation, or print, is marked by calm deliberation and a deep respect for things built to last.

You can find more of his works at his minimalist website: www.lolczyk.de

www.ingramcontent.com/pod-product-compliance
Lightning Source LLC
Chambersburg PA
CBHW061223240926
51846CB00006B/1330
* 9 7 8 3 9 1 2 1 4 7 0 4 9 *